Real SUCCESS

Real
SUCCESS

Feel Accomplished
and Find Fulfillment
in the
Modern World

Michelle Zawaski

NEW YORK

LONDON • NASHVILLE • MELBOURNE • VANCOUVER

Real SUCCESS
Feel Accomplished and Find Fulfillment in the Modern World

Published in New York, New York, by Morgan James Publishing in partnership with Difference Press. Morgan James is a trademark of Morgan James, LLC. www.MorganJamesPublishing.com

ISBN 978-1-64279-238-6 paperback
ISBN 978-1-64279-239-3 eBook
Library of Congress Control Number: 2018910389

Cover Design by:
Rachel Lopez
www.r2cdesign.com

Interior Design by:
Bonnie Bushman
The Whole Caboodle Graphic Design

In an effort to support local communities, raise awareness and funds, Morgan James Publishing donates a percentage of all book sales for the life of each book to Habitat for Humanity Peninsula and Greater Williamsburg.

Get involved today! Visit
www.MorganJamesBuilds.com

Dedication

To my daughter, Valerie,
Love leads, love inspires, love conquers.
You, my babydoll, are my inspiration.
May love always inspire you.
Always continue to shine your light.

Table of Contents

Introduction

You want to be successful right? Don't we all want that? I know I do.

Then you can be living the life all of us dream of, one of joy and fulfillment where you can experience life on your terms. You can be happy.

Janine always believed she would be successful. She worked hard to get the best grades she could in school, so that she could be granted more opportunity. She wanted to get into a great college so that she would be able to land her dream job. She saw herself landing an entry-level job in one of the top financial services companies in the world. She could start her career with a great base, learning from leaders in the field, while also taking home a paycheck that would prove her success. She did it all.

And she was so proud of herself. She accomplished what she set out to accomplish. She was a success.

She ended up spending her twenties working long hours and taking on extra responsibilities so that she could prove herself and move up the ladder. Work hard now to reap the benefits later, right? It worked—she has reaped many benefits. She has a great career and makes more than most of her peers. But now, as she is entering her mid-thirties, she is realizing that her social life is almost nonexistent outside of business networking events. Plus, she has yet to meet the partner that she longs for because, honestly, who has the time to date? She is getting older and feels as if life has just passed her by in a blur. As she walks into her apartment, at an early 9 p.m. end of the work day, she grabs a glimpse of the framed picture of her family on the shelving unit. She realizes she has not been able to spend one day with them in the last two months and she feels so far away from them at this moment. What happened?

"I am so close to my family and yet I feel like I don't even know what is happening with them. I really want to call my sister and catch up, but I am so exhausted, and I need to be up at 4 a.m. to get to the airport on time to catch the plane to Dallas tomorrow. I am doing everything I am supposed to be doing and I am successful. Why do I feel so alone and unfulfilled? I guess this is how it is," she says as she sets her alarm for the early wake-up and climbs into bed.

Janine has been sold the story, like most of us, that you work hard and sacrifice so that you will have all that you need later. As she is starting to realize that the last 15 years passed by in a blur, she is starting to question if this truly is the way it is supposed to be. Perhaps this question is coming up for you as well?

Do we really want to give up our time and energy now to reap benefits later? Is it ok to not nurture relationships now and hope that they will always be there for us later? Are we jeopardizing our health now to be secure financially? There must be a better way, right?

Maybe you feel like Janine. Have you been pushing forward on your path to success as you had been conditioned to believe? Have you done all the right things—everything you were supposed to do—and, on paper, you actually are largely successful? But are you realizing that there are holes in this lifestyle that you are living? Are you beginning to see big pieces that are missing, and are you starting to realize that life is passing you by without that feeling of fulfillment you expected and still desire?

I have created a life of accomplishment, happiness and success for myself by implementing the strategies I will present to you throughout this book. I have also had the opportunity to work with many others to support them on their quest and realization of their own real success. You also will achieve your real success if you follow through on what I will present to you.

Are you ready to truly start living life on your terms? Are you finally going to create the success and happiness you deserve?

In the next pages, I will show you how to finally begin to live the life that you deserve: one of accomplishment, fulfillment, happiness, and real success.

Chapter One
What is Real Success?

Ever since I can remember, I've had that fire in my belly. The one that told me I can do anything, if I just work for it. And I never questioned myself. I was supposed to do all of this, wasn't I? I was supposed to do the best I could at everything because it would get me to where I was supposed to be. I should always be striving for success, no? We all should always be striving for success, right?

But what is success?

I realized, at a certain point in my life, that I wasn't sure what success actually was. I was succeeding at many things, but I was not feeling fulfilled. Aren't fulfillment and happiness what we should be feeling when we are succeeding?

1

So, I took a step back and decided to start at the beginning. I looked up the meaning of success. Merriam-Webster's simple definition of success is 1. *the fact of getting or achieving wealth, respect, or fame* 2. *the correct or desired result of an attempt.*

So, they're telling me that wealth, respect, and fame are the only outcomes of success?

I am confused now.

I was raised understanding that success results in happiness, peace, and fulfillment. That's what I want! I do not want this constant feeling of busyness because there is always something bigger and better on the horizon. I have not even begun to enjoy the success I just achieved before I am striving to get to the next level.

So, I decided to stop.

I decided to reflect on what I truly felt that success meant for me in my heart.

What did I find?

I found that success to me is enjoying this life that I was given on earth. I have a short time here and I am extremely grateful for having been given the opportunity for my experience here. I don't want to just let it pass me by. I want to experience each moment, I want to enjoy each moment, and I want to grow with each moment. That is what my success is. Once I realized this, I decided to make it my reality. Of course, this reality still needs to be realistic. I need money to live. I cannot just walk around every day doing as I please, with my head in the clouds. And I still have that fire in my belly. I need to continue to honor that fire.

Easier said than done, right?

So, I now knew what I defined as success and I knew that I was going to get there. But how?

I was a single mom who needed to continue to provide stability and security to my daughter. I needed to accomplish more in the time I already had filled, and I needed to begin to honor myself in the process. I laughed at myself. Impossible! But the fire in the belly was still there and it said, "Michelle, you got this!" So, I forged ahead.

I realized that I needed to disconnect that fire from what my mind had learned to believe. That fire was driving me along with society and the "norms" I was conditioned to believe. Now I needed to reconnect that fire to what my heart desires and I would be able to continue to honor it, just on a different path: a path to my own definition of success.

This is not easy. Beliefs are conditioned in us from society, caregivers, teachers, and peers, among others. As soon as we begin to sway from these beliefs, we begin to fight ourselves. Our mind works in tandem with what our beliefs are, whether we are conscious of them or not. Our desires are not always connected to these beliefs but are coming from our emotional and physical wants and needs. This creates a disconnect that is not always seen for what it is but rather creates anxiety, stress, tension, and confusion. Most often we stay on the path we are on because our beliefs have us stuck here. If we try to sway from them the mind will continually question what we are doing. Without full, conscious awareness of what is happening it becomes easier to continue as we were, assuming that by doing so the stress and confusion will subside.

But there must be a way to start living our own definition of success, right?

Yes, there is, and I am excited to say I have found a way and I am eager and willing to help you to accomplish this yourself. In the following pages, I will show you ways to embrace the possible and finally begin living your real success. And by the way, there is not just one way that works for all of us. We are all unique, and we will all design our own destinies. I have a process that will help you to find your own unique way to proceed.

In order to begin we must decide what your definition of real success is.

If you are able at this moment (if not, then set time aside to do this later) I would like you to pick up a pen and paper.

We all have areas of our lives where we feel we are already successful and areas where perhaps we are not yet.

First, write a list of areas where you do feel you are a success. Perhaps when you think of overall relationships you do not feel that you are fully a success; however, you have an awesome relationship with your sister. Then you will write "relationship with sister" as a success. You can, and should, get as detailed as possible to ensure you are including all of your successes.

Second, start a new list of areas that are not yet completely successful, but that you would like to become so. For example, while you have a great relationship with your sister, the relationship you have with your brother is not yet at that level, although you would like it to be. So "relationship with brother" can go on the not-yet-a-success list. Again, take your time, and get as detailed as possible.

Once you have the two lists complete, I want you to go down each one and write down the first word(s) that come up when you ask yourself, "How does this make me feel?" When I say, "How does the relationship with my sister make me feel?" for example, I can write awesome, loved, enthusiastic. When I ask how the relationship with my brother makes me feel, I may write stressed, tense, sad. Take your time to do this and be honest with yourself.

Once complete, go back, one more time, to your not-yet-a-success list and ask yourself, "What feeling does this need to change to for me to be able to move it to my success list?"

Now go back down your list of feelings, the already-a-success feelings that you have in your life as well as the feelings on your not-yet-a-success list that need to change to for you to remove them from this list.

Are there underlying feelings that come up more than once on your list?

Are any interconnected?

See if there are any patterns or any feelings that come up often. These most likely are very important to you. Or, perhaps, there is no specific pattern, but as you read through the feelings, you resonate more strongly with some.

Finally, what are the 3–5 feelings that would make you feel the way you want to and deserve to if you had them in almost everything you do each day?

Write these 3–5 feelings down.

To feel these feelings daily is your *real success*.

What is your *real success*?

Chapter Two
What You Need First

*J*anine finally reached a point where she was no longer able to continue pushing away the questions she had about why she felt so unfulfilled. She was the maid of honor in her sister's wedding and she was longing to enjoy the weekend with her family, surrounded by love and joy. She needed to be at the rehearsal dinner Thursday night. Friday she would spend the day with her sister at a spa, relaxing and catching up. Saturday was the big event. It was planned for months. Her flight was early Thursday morning and at 4 p.m. on Wednesday afternoon, her boss called her into her office. The company was up against a wall. Sudden changes with a client were now leaving Janine's team 24 hours to meet a new critical deadline. She knew Janine had the wedding, but they really needed her to work the next 24 hours, and honestly, she was giving Janine no other option.

Janine walked away with tears rolling down her face. How can this be more important than her own sister's once-in-a-lifetime day? But what could Janine do? She really had no other options. She picked up the phone and called her sister. She would move her flight to late Thursday night, so she could still make the spa day and, of course, the wedding. Her sister could hear the emotion in Janine's voice and told her all that mattered was that she was ok and that she should do what she needed to—if she was there for the Saturday event, all would be ok.

Janine worked hard and long to accomplish what had to be accomplished over the next 24 hours, but it was not the same as the hundreds of times it had occurred in the past. Something had changed in her—she could feel it. She was emotional the entire time. She knew that she should be with her family now, not here. This was Janine's turning point. She knew she had to do something. She had no idea what, but she did know she was going to figure it out and do it, just like she always had in all areas of her life before.

Do you know what changed for Janine? Her motivation. She was always motivated, and always accomplishing, but up until this point a paycheck and a title had been her motivation. Now her world seemed so out of place. This success that she had already achieved was no longer fulfilling her. She knew she needed more. She was tired of seeing life pass by so quickly. She knew she needed friends and family, possibly a significant other, love, companionship, and an added level of fulfillment. Life is too short to just work hard. She was craving some down time, and some play time, on her terms. If she could accomplish this, she would find so many things. She would find personal satisfaction and success at her level, not just on paper. She would reignite her purpose. She would feel well-rounded and accomplished. She would create space for herself and for love and fulfillment at another level from what she had allowed herself to have prior.

What can you gain? You are reading this book because something pulled you to it. What will you have if you finally can feel your real success?

Janine was gaining love, space for herself, and overall time.

I reignited my passion and purpose, and re-inspired myself in what I had to give back to this world. Maybe you can gain self-love and confidence. Or perhaps you are truly happy with your family and home-life, as well as your career, and you realize you just need to gain back time and energy. We all can gain. We all can grow. We all can have success and fulfillment.

Janine changed her motivation and moved forward. I changed my motivation and I grew to my next level. You as well can change your motivation and move forward on your path.

You need motivation to move forward in creating your real success. Without this motivation and drive, you will not get to the level of real success that you deserve and desire.

Let's take some time to look at what motivation is for you.

In the last chapter, you decided what your real success is. Now, take some time to ask yourself:

- Right now, what is holding you back from this real success?
- Why have you not achieved it yet?

It is easier to just stay with the status quo. Life becomes habitual and we get into schedules and once we realize we really would like to feel differently, we can end up blocked by fears, anxieties, excuses. But what happens when we do not ignite the small fire that starts to burn in our belly? When we do not move forward we can build up stress, overwhelm, and discontent. This all can lead to sickness if we let it continue. We also can lose ourselves in the process, and our inspiration, drive, and purpose get suppressed to a point that we no longer can remember what actually drives us.

- What is not achieving your real success doing to you?

Now, let's go a step further.

- What does life look like for you when you fully achieve your real success?
- What will happen?

As you answer these questions, really connect with your own truth. Explore them in detail, to truly understand where you are and where you can be and deserve to be.

Now, finally look again at:

- What does life look like for you when you are not achieving your real success?
- Are you ok with staying here?
- What does life look like for you when you fully achieve your real success?
- Is there any other option than getting here?

In truly connecting to these questions, have you come to a conclusion? Is staying where you are an option? Or is the only option to create real success? If real success is your only option then you feel the fire in your belly to create it. That fire is your motivation.

Keep your answers to these questions accessible to you so you can refer to them whenever you need to reconnect with your motivation.

Janine realized that if she did not focus on her own definition of success, she would just continue the path that she was on, and 5, 10, 20 years would pass her by in a flash—leaving her still feeling stressed, overworked, alone, and unfulfilled. For her to knowingly allow that to happen was not an option. She dedicated herself to finding a way to overcome this. The only future she could allow was one that was filled with love and relationships, space for herself and time. Janine had found her motivation.

I realized at a point in my life that I was talking myself into being happy. On paper I was. And when I was saying to myself that I was happy, I was allowing my mind to truly believe it. My subconscious knew, however, and it was able to send me the necessary signs to shift my thought process and re-motivate myself. As soon as that happened, I had too much to lose. I needed to take steps to shift myself to a new level. I could only live my life in my view of true happiness. I gave myself no other choice.

So, ask yourself:

- What will happen if you do not create your real success right now?
- Are you ok with that happening?
- If you do not create your real success now, then when will you?

If, as you asked yourself these questions, you concluded that achieving your real success now is the only answer, congratulations! You are motivated and driven to begin creating it. Your vision of what your life will become and the fact that it cannot stay as it is, is your motivation. Your future is in your power to shape. You have decided to be the captain of your life.

If, instead, you are still unsure, have excuses as to why you cannot deal with this now, or believe that you need to stay where you are because of a belief or responsibility, you are not motivated. If this is you, you will not achieve your real success. If you do not believe that living your real success is your only option, you will block yourself from creating and achieving it. Only motivation will drive you to move out of your rut and into real success.

If you are motivated and ready to gain self-fulfillment and personal success, then you will find ways in the next chapters.

You will gain insight to what types of steps you can take to move yourself forward.

Questions to Find Your Motivation:

- What does life look like for you when you are not achieving your real success?
- Are you ok with staying here?
- What does life look like for you when you fully achieve your real success?
- Is there any other option than getting here?

Write down your Motivation:

Chapter Three
What's Happening

Sandy and Laura both came to me searching for an escape from the overwhelm they felt in their daily lives. Sandy was in her late forties and just newly married. She had a job in a very toxic environment and she also had her elderly mom living with her, so that she could care for her. She really wanted to create a process to help her and her husband to enjoy more time together while also allowing herself more time to take care of herself. She was constantly running, always taking care of everyone else. But she was unable to release anything because this was all part of what she had to do. She had to work to support herself and her family. She had to spend time with her husband to nurture this great new life they were beginning, and she had to take care of her elderly mother. What gives?

Laura wanted a similar outcome. She was a 40-year-old single mom. She was a teacher and fitness instructor. She cared deeply about what type of mother she was. She wanted to ensure she made the right choices for herself and her child so that she raised a healthy, compassionate, and loving soul. She also had to be there completely for all the children's lives she was nurturing through teaching. She was passionate, as well, about her fitness clients who she was helping achieve their passions and life goals. She always had to be on, but she was constantly worried about everyone else and not herself. She became emotionally and physically exhausted trying to keep up. But this is what she had to do! How could she not?

Both Sandy and Laura were exhausted trying to keep up with what they believed was right. They were giving up their own time, energy, and self-nourishment to give back to others because they would never think otherwise. They were doing what was right. They both were also getting to a breaking point. They knew something needed to change so that they could continue to be there for others like they should be. Both were looking for the same end result, but each needed to reach it in very different ways.

Sandy was able to add very small steps into her day that did not take any time away from her responsibilities. These steps were placed in to help her to refocus on what was in front of her. She was able to get more done in less time, and she began to offer more time to herself—to nurture what she wanted—rather than always focusing on what those around her needed.

Laura was at a different stage. She had already started work on herself and was at a point where she saw connections to the beliefs that she knew were driving her, and she was not sitting well with them, because she knew that the beliefs were not authentically hers. This was causing incessant chatter in her head and driving some emotional breakdowns that she knew she needed to free herself of. Laura was able to add some steps into her life to allow her to break her chains to her mind chatter and allow her to more consciously live and feel her emotions. Then she could become Laura again and not just a caregiver to those around her.

Each of these women wanted a similar outcome. Each were unique individuals at different places in their lives. Each needed to create a plan that resonated with and would work for them. They succeeded in getting to their next level because they were able to do what they needed to do to get there. They used my guidance and support to get them there more easily and more quickly than they would have on their own. They were able to create lasting change by creating a plan that worked for them individually.

So, what does success mean to you? What does fulfillment feel like?

Janine thought success was work hard, play later. She was passionate about having a successful career and assumed this success would just naturally lead to fulfillment.

I had a daughter that was pure love and light. We moved on by ourselves so that she could be provided for in an environment of love and stability. I truly felt I had made great decisions to support us. But something was still not sitting right, something was still not fulfilled.

We all were doing everything we believed we were supposed to be doing—but something was still missing. Perhaps you feel like Janine, Sandy, Laura, and myself. Perhaps you are truly happy with your hard work, determination, and motivation. Or you are confident that you live following your inspirations and passions, yet you still can't help but feel like there could be an even better way.

One common thread I have come across in all the people I have worked with is that they all believe they were following the path they were supposed to in order to get ahead and achieve success. If we are all doing what we are supposed to do, then why do so many of us get to a point in our lives where we feel as if there should be more? What is preventing us from that feeling of total fulfillment? We are successful (on paper). We are smart, driven, and hard-working. There have been millions before us that have taught us that this is the way. How could they all have gotten it wrong? Or are we just the ones who are getting it wrong?

When we are born into this world, we are all born as pure love. There are no expectations. Our world around us (society, family, culture, religion) teaches us what is expected of us. These expectations develop within us as we grow and learn. They become a part of us.

All groups (society, cultures, etc.) have written and unwritten rules. These have developed over time for numerous reasons. Most of all, they developed because they helped bring order and overall understanding. Also, the human mind likes reason, and this showed us that there were "good" ways to live. Generations of people helped form this conditioning that we all live with in some way today. These expectations are our guide to overall "good."

But what is this good that I talk about? Who decided that the overall good was also right for each individual?

What does this "good" mean to you?

Each and every one of us will have different responses to that question. We will all have these differences in feelings and opinions because we are all unique, individual people. Each one of us has experienced a different mix of conditioning in our lifetimes. We also are all unique enough to process similar conditioning in different ways. So, if we are all individuals learning and processing uniquely, then how can an overall expectation fit for all of us?

It doesn't.

So, what do we do?

Most of us just keep on going. We continue to do what we are supposed to do because it is the "good" thing to do. We have also been promised that it is the right thing to do and when we do what's right, we end up on top.

What is this top? Success? But we already saw that success is not the same to each of us. So, if we are all striving for success by doing the same things, then we would not be able to reach the same point and all feel fulfilled.

Where do we go now?

We can't very well go against everything we have been taught, all that is ingrained in ourselves, can we? What if we did? *Stop it!*

Now you're just getting me scared, exhilarated, anxious... I am not sure how I feel! This brings up so many thoughts, so many feelings.

Well, what if I told you there is a way? There is a way to stop settling for what you are *told* will satisfy you and start living with what *you* know will satisfy you. And the way is not throwing away all this conditioning just like that. It does not have to be scary or chaotic.

I really honed in on this process myself when I hit my turning point. When I decided once and for all that I was going to start living my life as my authentic self rather than as the person I thought I was supposed to be. That turning point brought it all to the forefront for me. It allowed me to consciously see that I had subconsciously created techniques and tools—for myself and others over the years—that created shifts in each of us individually to push us up to the next level. Each of us is at a different personal level, and that is the level we are breaking from. So, there is no epiphany process, no one-shot deal for all of us. We are each in need of something different. The Real Success Strategy is based on that: that each of us has our own next step, and that step is not going to be the same for me as it is for the person sitting next to me.

Although we are all unique individuals, and each of us need to reach our next level in different ways, the tools and techniques that can be used to reach our authentic success do fall into some overall concepts. I will take you through these in the next chapters of this book, so that you can see for yourself where you can personally relate to them, and how you too can create lasting change for yourself.

Chapter Four

The Real Success Strategy

*Y*ou now should have taken the time to understand what your personal real success consists of. Let's begin to move forward to make this real success your reality. Perhaps you are doing what is expected of you, what your family expects, what your society expects, and what you expect of yourself. We have begun to see how these expectations create lives based on influences and learnings rather than our own true identity.

So how, after so many years and with so many deeply rooted beliefs, do you finally begin to honor yourself?

Janine decided to start honoring herself once she hit her breaking point. She finally got to a point where she realized that she was missing things in her life that would create fulfilment.

Once she was aware of this, she decided that these missing things were more important to her than staying where she was, and this created her motivation to find a way to get to her ideal.

Sandy was creating a new beginning for herself with her new marriage and was so excited to see where life would now take her. She had so many responsibilities on her plate, however, that she became exhausted and overwhelmed. She knew she wanted to pursue the life she was dreaming of, but felt held back due to time and energy. She knew something had to change so that she could feel as alive and joyful as she deserved to be. This awareness brought her to a realization that living *as she deserved* was the only way she could see herself in the future, and this became her motivation. Now there was no turning back.

To finally begin to honor ourselves, as discussed in Chapter Two, we need motivation. Motivation is the driving force for change. Once we create motivation, we will move ourselves forward.

What about you? Are you just plain exhausted? Are you physically and/or emotionally drained? Is life passing you by in a blur and you just want it to stop and slow down? Maybe some of this resonates with you, possibly all of it does. What if none of it does and you actually feel great about everything you are doing and everything you have accomplished, yet you do feel that there is something still missing? You may not even know what it actually is that is missing, but you cannot deny that you feel something is off.

If you stay where you are and just keep on going what will happen? Will you go through life always with these feelings? Will you just fight these feelings and push them down as you continue on your life path? Maybe they will just continue to grow and create misery. Maybe they will be suppressed and allow you to keep living as you always have but, subconsciously, start to make you sick, preventing you from physically continuing your status quo.

What is the motivation you created back in Chapter Two?

Motivation will drive you. It will drive you to make shifts within yourself to ensure you do not end up with the outcome you do not desire. Motivation is what you will lean on when you are tired, stressed, and overwhelmed. It will pull you back up to continue.

Once you are motivated, the next step is making a choice. You need to make the choice that best serves you. What do you need to do to serve the motivation you just created? Are you choosing to take steps to change your outcome? If you are choosing to change the outcome, how are you going to do it? What is your next step?

Before I share the overall strategy with you, I want to lay the groundwork. There is one method that will incorporate itself into every area I share with you throughout the book. This method is what I call the three As. The three As method, once implemented, will assist you in making every moment meaningful. In everything that you do, these three As will apply. The three As are:

Awareness

Acceptance

Allowance

Awareness: Here we begin to see what is actually happening. We pay attention to exactly what is in front of us either physically, emotionally, or mentally. As I am walking down the street, *I am fully aware that it is a crisp fall day and the leaves are falling from the trees.* As I am going about my day, *I become aware that emotionally I feel tense and irritable. My body is tight, and I am feeling stress.* As I sit at my desk, *I am aware that mentally I am going over what needs to be accomplished today since I am facing a deadline and need to get it accomplished swiftly.* Creating the awareness in every moment will allow us to see what is actually happening. It keeps us from staying in the past or moving forward to the future and brings clarity to what we can affect right now.

The question we should ask ourselves to create this awareness in any situation is:

What is happening right now?

Acceptance: Once we create the awareness, we now need to accept it. Accepting it means that we understand that this is our current reality. We are aware that this is real—whether we like it or not. Whether we agree with it or not. *The air is crisp and cool. I need to be wearing a jacket to stay warm.* This is true. *I feel irritated. This irritation is because I am annoyed that I am running late for an important appointment.* This is true. The thought coming into my head is, *I have to finish this project now! I have to complete this project, reply to emails, take a client call and be at a meeting at 3!* This is true.

At this point the question we ask:

Is this true? Or is this real?

Allowance: Now we are aware of what is happening, and we have accepted it as our current reality. At this point, we must allow it. Allowing it is understanding our reality, and creating compassion for it—whether we like the reality or not—so that we can move past it. *It's cool and crisp and I am wearing a jacket. I would rather it be warm and be wearing sandals.* But this is my reality. I have accepted it. Now I can enjoy it. *As much as I love summer, this day is actually beautiful in its own way. I love the colors of all the leaves. The crisp air makes me feel alive.* Or, *Yes, I am irritated because I am running late. I am running late because I was in worse than expected traffic. I cannot change this now. I know I have done what I could to arrive in better time, but things occurred outside of my control. I will get to the appointment and hopefully all will work out, regardless of my tardiness. Yes, I hear you, thought, that I need to finish this project now. I know I am on a deadline, so I understand why you are nagging me and I appreciate you keeping me in line. However, I need to focus on the task at hand right now, not have a conversation with you.*

The question to ask here is:

How do I allow this truth to have space here?

Awareness = Observing what is within you and around you
Acceptance = Recognizing that this is reality
Allowance = Compassionate understanding of the reality

These three As will help you in any situation and I will continue to apply these as I next show you the overall concepts/areas that will help you become closer to your own authentic real success. Possibly these will fit into what you believe your next step should be. Some of these you may feel are already a part of your life and some you may feel are not. As we discussed, we are all on our own levels and those levels always have room to grow and evolve.

The Real Success Strategy consists of:

1. Everyday Small Steps:

Here, without changing your current routine, you are able to add small steps into your routine as you go through your day, so that you can create more time and energy without taking any physical time away from your already hectic schedule and life. Maybe you already have some of this process intertwined into your everyday life but are not consciously aware of it. Or possibly, you are consciously aware of the small moments, but have not realized that you can expand this into all steps within your day. This is a process—that I will expand on in the next chapter—of becoming aware of what works for you and taking small, consistent steps to add more of this back into your everyday routine in small ways until you end up with this naturally. Just as our minds can be conditioned by outside influences, here you are training yourself to be conditioned back to your natural state while continuing to live a life within the social structures that you reside in.

Once you are able to live your current routine like this, you are able to begin to enjoy and experience your moments more fully. The 3 As will become natural to you and no longer need to be thought about specifically. As this starts to take hold over larger amounts of your time, you also begin to see things in a different light than you may have prior to this adjustment. Then you start to move into the next stages.

2. Priorities:

You will start to adjust your energy as you become more aware of the moments you are experiencing. You will start to reconnect to yourself as you develop a new knowledge toward your place in the world. You will see how you need to take care of yourself first, and foremost, to be able to give back fully to the people you love and to the world as a whole. This will help you to re-prioritize your life—enabling you to lead the life you desire.

Once you are able to reset your priorities you will move on to:

3. Breakthrough

As you go through the previous stages and become more connected to and aware within your moments, you will begin to question your thoughts and emotions. You may start to see your beliefs and conditionings differently than you had in the past and you will have new emotions come up because of that. Your mind chatter will evolve and change as well. For some, your incessant thoughts will be on overdrive as you start to change to your natural state of being, because of the expectations you had placed on yourself that are now evolving. All of these are what I call barriers to our breakthrough. These barriers are a part of all of us and are largely a part of our conditioning leading up to this point. Just as with all else, these will be different for each person and will come up at different intensities and in different forms for each of us. Whenever these barriers come up, there are tools and techniques that can be used to break them down. These are what I call Small Steps to Breakthrough.

Once you are able to shift your everyday life, re-prioritize, and break through your barriers, you are able to see yourself in a new light. You are now getting onto the same page with you. You can now put all that you have taught yourself into play to start living life where you are authentically successful— successful on your terms. Many of us can continue to have beliefs and conditionings from our past that we would like to keep, as they feel authentic to us. Some others will shed many of these. There is no right answer as there is no one right way for everyone. You will evolve at your own speed and pace because that is what you choose to do.

In the following pages, I will delve deeper into these overall concepts of the strategy so that you can see in more detail how they may fit for you.

Questions to Achieve the 3 As:

- Awareness: What is happening right now?
- Acceptance: Is this true? Or is this real?
- Allowance: How do I allow this truth to have space here?

Chapter Five
Everyday Small Steps

Most of us lead full lives. Full schedules. We always have something that needs to be dealt with that is next on our list. We go through our days thinking about how we are going to get it all done. Many of us will think about our work deadlines or routines as we are trying to watch tv at night with our family, or as we shower in the morning, or even as we are commuting to work. Once we arrive at work, we think about what needs to be dealt with at home. *What should we have for dinner tonight? Oh, I have Crystal's birthday this weekend—I need to get a gift. The soccer game is Thursday—I need to make sure the uniform is clean and ready to go.* As we do this to ourselves, are we accomplishing anything? Running over to-do lists in our heads does not get the to-dos checked off. Actually, as we were mulling over the work to-dos last night, we did not realize that we missed our child trying to tell us that they had an exciting day because they were rewarded for being a great listener. As we were thinking about what to have for dinner tonight, we could have already completed the project we were working on and not fallen even further behind schedule at work.

If we stopped and we paid more attention to what was in front of us, we would see more, hear more, experience more, become more efficient, and create more time and energy for ourselves.

Stopped!? How could we stop thinking? It's human nature to think! And if we weren't thinking, how could we remember everything that had to get done?

Actually, it is the mind's nature to think. It is the soul's nature to know. The mind is a great tool, but just like many things, if used in excess, it can do more harm than good. We think because it makes us feel as if we have control. You have control over your life, right? Your thoughts are helping you to make the right choices? Well, actually, these thoughts are often controlling us. The thinking begins to take over and drive us. As we lessen these thoughts, we start to gain back our control. In the end, we only have control over the actions we take in the moment we are in. Thinking about what happened yesterday, and mulling over what we could have done, won't change anything. Thinking about what to have for dinner tonight, and how we really need to fix that faucet that started to drip, will not magically make those things happen for us. But looking at what is right in front of us, in the moment we are in, allows us to gain back our control. We can focus on the now and make a choice *right then* that will make a difference in us immediately. Making a difference right now allows for new opportunities to present themselves. Suddenly, what we are making for dinner later is not even a concern. It will be a concern once it is a priority, of course, but we can learn to let it be until we are in that specific moment. By doing so, we start to refocus ourselves throughout the day. This refocus creates more time. When we focus on a task in front of us, without distraction, we start to get more accomplished in less time. These small steps are training us to create awareness (The 3 As from Chapter Three) in everything that we do.

Easier said than done, I know. We have also become conditioned to think. We end up talking more to ourselves than to anyone else in our lifetime. And that thinking, and talking to ourselves, can lead to burnout if allowed to run its own course with no boundaries. So, what can be done?

If we decide right this moment that we want to run a 15k race, do we sign up today to run 10 miles tomorrow? No, we need to train first, because our bodies would not be able to just perform out of the blue. Once we decide that our goal is to run a 15k, we come up with a training plan and we build ourselves up to running that distance. We start out at the pace our body can handle, we push ourselves, and each day, we accomplish more. This is the same process we use when we want to train our mindset. We cannot just flip a switch and start living this way fully. We need to take it one step at a time, be consistent, and build ourselves up to take on more and more. These are the small steps that we begin to take. We decide on the first step and we incorporate it into our day. We repeat this step consistently, so that our brain becomes so accustomed to it that it becomes a natural process for us. As we start to incorporate the first step into our lives, we can then add another step into the mix. This builds up until we naturally live in this new state. The new mindset moves from a conscious choice to a subconscious rule.

So what type of steps can we take to start shifting our everyday being?

When working with clients, I like to first ask them to reflect on when in their lives are they not thinking. *Hmmm. Aren't I always thinking?* Well, is there an activity that you take part in, where you truly feel calm and peaceful while in the process? A time when you are not in a stream of constant thoughts, but rather just lost in what is happening?

This can be many different things for many different people. Stacy, a client of mine, found that she "lost herself" when she was in the presence of children. She had always loved being with children and now she was realizing why. She could completely place all of her attention on children when she was with them. She realized she always stayed in the moment when she was with kids. She played with them and she stopped thinking. She would leave a room filled with children feeling satisfied, calm, and peaceful. For others, even the thought of a room full of children causes a sense of chaos and overwhelm. That's ok. This was Stacy's way and that's what mattered.

I personally found, since a very young age, that art was my escape. I would lose myself for hours in an art project and I would walk away feeling refreshed, accomplished, and relaxed. For many years, I even mistook this love for art as possibly being my purpose. I felt so great being creative, that I saw it as a passion, and possibly a path I should take in my life to fulfill my purpose. As I developed and grew more, I realized that this wasn't the case and rather, that this was a form of escape for me. When you are living your purpose, you will also associate the same feelings and emotions with that; however, we could have more than one way that resonates with us as a form of escape.

Others I have worked with have realized their natural state of peace was when they journaled, read, played an instrument, or danced. Some find it when they are interacting with large groups of people, yet others can accomplish peace through total solitude and meditation. There are multitudes of ways that work for different types of people.

Hopefully, this has helped you to begin to think of ways that you may already find your state of peace in your daily routine. Take some time to reflect on when this happens for you. How do you feel when you allow yourself to experience this state?

Now how can we get that feeling more consistently, in our everyday activities and not just when we are performing that one specific calming action?

Once you understand what you want to feel like, in every moment of every day, we can figure out new steps to expand it to other areas and times of your day.

So, what does your daily routine consist of? For me, I was a mom and a business executive in NYC. I would wake up, shower, and get my daughter up, fed, and dressed while I made lunches for both of us. Once her bus picked her up, I would travel into NYC via train and I had a ten-minute walk to my office from the train. A great first step for me was to ensure that when I walked from the train to my office, I would take in and focus on my surroundings completely. I made sure to pay attention to the sky. *What color was it? Clouds or no clouds? General weather? Birds?* Also, I started to pay closer attention to the people walking past me, the cars, the stores, and the buildings I was passing. I took this ten minutes of my day and I consciously decided to change my mindset in this fraction of my routine. It was not a flawless process. I would sometimes find myself thinking of what I needed to do as soon as I arrived to work, or by the end of my day at the office. I sometimes would begin to think of what occurred last night when my mother had called to talk. But as these thoughts came in, I was able to be completely aware of it, then I would accept the thought and tell myself, *I understand that these are things that my mind would like to think about, but right now I need to return my awareness to this moment I am in.* This would allow me to return to my process without causing myself undue stress. I did not want to get angry at myself because I was unable to just take these ten minutes and not think. I am human, and I will only change if I am compassionate to myself first. Once I was able to experience these ten minutes of each day in this state, without resistance, I would add a new step into my routine. As I consciously added steps in, I was subconsciously adjusting my being and I started to see that I found myself in this state more and more without even realizing it. I felt less stress and more energized. I was getting more done without even changing my schedule. And best of all, time was not passing by as quickly. I started to enjoy even more of the mundane, and I truly appreciated each moment on a new level—a level of deeper fulfillment.

When Sandy and I first started working together, she was motivated to adjust herself so that she would be able to enter each part of her day with an open mind. She had found that she had so much going on that it was hard to not carry her workday into her time caring for her mom, and then her time caring for mom into her time to spend with her husband. She was very aware of this, but she was unable to pinpoint ways to stop it from happening. One of the first steps she decided to add into her routine was during her 15-minute drive from work to Mom's. She always listened to the radio in the car on the way. She had a habit of putting on talk shows, so she could catch up on news and world happenings. She realized that by doing so, she would leave her office worked up over the toxic environment she was in and put herself into another environment that caused her to stay on that level. The talk and news would change her focus but not her emotional state. She made a conscious choice to put music on. She had no idea what would happen, but she had to try and she did.

A week later, she was surprised and excited about what a difference this was already making for her. She couldn't completely explain it, but she was feeling more relaxed and felt as if she was able to unwind a bit. This allowed her to go into caring for her mom in a calmer state. She felt as if she was with her mom more. And she also was surprised at how it seemed to affect her overall day. Just allowing herself this time, for 15 minutes a day, seemed to be allowing her to feel calmer during other parts of her day as well. This was just the beginning and one very small step that was making a larger shift in her well-being. She was so excited and motivated to keep moving forward.

Sounds very simple right? Once again, it's different for each of us and the process is very important. Sandy was able to add one simple step into her routine and stick to just that for a week before she was ready to add another small step in. I added my ten-minute walk into my routine, but I did not add another just a week later. I needed to stay with that step for longer before adding in another. We live in a fast-paced world where we all expect a certain immediacy; however, when we push too fast, sometimes we can create a longer overall process for ourselves. If I quickly added another step in—prior to truly accomplishing the first one—I would start creating overwhelm rather than calm. We need to feel completely comfortable with the first step, before we can add the next step.

As you saw with both myself and Sandy, once we were truly comfortable, we felt as if that tiny portion of our day was already creating change for us in other parts. Once we added more steps in, as we were ready for them, we created even more change over our days. Each of us will create this change at a different pace and that is ok. We need to make the choices that will move us forward. Once we let our minds start to decide how fast we want this accomplished, we will pull ourselves off track.

Maybe you are reading this and saying, "I completely know what my first step needs to be and I am going to start it tomorrow." Good for you! You can do this, we all can do this, just make sure you allow yourself the time you need as well. Many of you can do this all on your own. Many of you will need some support and direction. Accept what works for you and honor it.

This process seems simple, but it is life-changing! This is the first step toward giving yourself back control. Once you are able to add in all the steps you need to shift to the next level, you will see a dramatic difference in yourself, physically, emotionally, and mentally. You are beginning to seize your moments. Remember your routine is still the same—the same hectic chaos that you were dealing with before—yet you feel calmer, steadier, and more in control.

Now you feel as if you are handling your days with more ease. You still may feel you have too much on your overall plate and you may even still feel a certain level of overwhelm—albeit it feels slightly better than before. You feel more accomplished and fulfilled but you may not be at your top level of fulfillment and personal success. That's ok. This is the first step and for many, once they shift to this level they will see so many more opportunities for themselves and start to move toward those opportunities. In the next pages, I will continue to show you how to continue bringing yourself closer to your level of real success.

What is your first *everyday small step?*

Chapter Six

The Priorities

Rose is a mother and grandmother, first and foremost. She married and had children young. Her life has always revolved around her family. She was supposed to get married and have a family—that is what she believed since she could remember. She loved every second of it. At least she believed she loved every second of it, until she realized she never knew who she actually was. By giving herself completely to her loved ones, she never nurtured herself. She found herself in her late fifties never knowing what she wanted or what brought her joy. She spent all of her time and energy focused on what everyone else needed and while she was doing it, she truly felt it was right. Now, as her children are adults and having children of their own, she is starting to see that she may have given too much. She began to see that perhaps she even caused her own children, whom she loved with every ounce of her soul, some hardships because she had always done too much for them. She took away some of their independence in doing so, and she now could see how this was affecting their adult lives. This realization also brought to her attention how far away she felt from herself. She was working so hard to be the perfect mom all of her life that she did not know who Rose was. She was realizing that by never nurturing Rose, she had lost herself and she had also taken away a piece of independence for each of her children when she decided to do everything for them.

What Rose was now doing was revisiting her priorities. She always wanted to be the perfect mom. Now she was aware that she still wanted to be the perfect mom, but that her view of what a perfect mom was had changed. Her new version of a perfect mom was one where she could better serve her children and grandchildren by shifting to a role of mentor rather than problem solver. She now could see that she had to get to this new role—there was no way she could stay as she was. She had her motivation. However, although Rose was widely aware of where she needed to be in the end, the process to get there was not so clear.

Knowing the end point but not knowing what steps to take to get there can be overwhelming. This is how Rose now felt. She spent the last 50 years with the beliefs she was now trying to change. Her actions and reactions were more habit to her than actual, thought-out choices. Rose's love for her family, however, motivated her enough to dedicate herself to figuring this out.

Rose realized that she needed to start doing things for Rose. She knew if she could do this, she would help herself to realize truly who she was, and she also would start to help her children in different ways. She realized that she had conditioned them to depend on her for most things, and if she could now make herself a priority, she could possibly take steps that would help them to lessen that dependence on her. This was not an easy step for Rose. She was so conditioned to believe that she needed to be there for everyone else, first and foremost, that even the thought of making choices for herself was a struggle.

Many people see prioritizing themselves as selfish. We are taught to take care of others first. When we are hired for a job we "need" to do what our boss asks of us, like it or not. Otherwise, we will not have a job. There are social conditionings that tell us that we also should be taking care of others before ourselves. Customers always come first. Children always need to be taken care of because they cannot provide for themselves. Parents took care of us, so once we children are of adult age, we should be caring for them. And the list goes on.

Where does that leave you?

From the sound of it, it leaves you last.

As Rose realized, once she would be able to make herself a priority, she could start shifting herself into the new reality she was pursuing. The same is true for all of us. If you truly want to live life feeling real success, you will need to make yourself your first priority.

Now are you asking why must I be the top priority? And how can I do this? Let me show you.

We all have a laundry list of to-dos each day and every single check box is next to an important step that needs to be completed. What makes one step higher on the totem pole than the next? A work deadline is important because you need to accomplish it in order to prove yourself at the office—or at the least you cannot jeopardize your career by not getting it done. That would also jeopardize your financial standing and security for yourself and possibly your family. But getting to the gym and eating healthy are two more boxes that should be priority, because your health needs to come first—otherwise, you would not be able to do any of these to-dos. Oh, but wait your children are the #1 priority since you are their caregiver and confidant. You need to make sure you are raising them right. Your daughter needs supplies for the science project due this week and you also need to be at your son's baseball game this evening to cheer him on. Dinner is important because of course your family needs to be nourished and healthy. And the list can go on and on. What makes one step a priority over another? All of this needs to get done. You need to take care of everything to support yourself and your family. You need to keep doing it all because that is what you are supposed to do.

As we talked about, when our lives and minds are clogged up with what needs to get done, we are allowing time to pass by quickly and we are allowing all of these priorities to control our days. Now what will happen if you add a constant top priority to your list? What happens when you make that top priority *you*?

The statement of putting yourself first may, at first glance, feel selfish and greedy. You may feel anxious or scared about considering yourself as the top priority. Doing this may go against what you have been taught. I am supposed to be "good" and "good" means taking care of my loved ones and the world around me, first and foremost. Aren't I supposed to be the perfect worker, the perfect parent, the perfect friend? Once I am able to do it all—and do it all right—I will be a success. I will be leaned on and loved as I crave to be. But what if I told you that by putting yourself first, you actually create more space for all of these to-dos in your life? What if, by putting yourself first, you realize you are able to give more back to the world than you had been doing all along?

When you decide to put yourself first, you make a choice to live authentically. You can nurture yourself, which in turn gives back more to the world. As you become the priority, you start to make choices based on what is right for you at that moment, not what is right for the rest of the world. You don't know what is right for the world—you only know what is right for you. If you make choices because you think it is what you are supposed to choose, you end up in the same vicious cycle of stress, overwhelm, frustration, and under-fulfillment. Once in this cycle, you pass along these feelings to whomever you are dealing with. When you put yourself first and foremost, you end up with more clarity, peace, and fulfillment. These feelings help to put you into a mindset that allows you to give more to the person whom you are with at the moment.

Personally, I know that I need my sleep. Sleep is very important for me. Once I sleep, my whole day is easier, calmer, and more productive. Now, as I said, I am a single mom working full time and building a business. I have a lot on my plate, but I know I will always have a lot on my plate so I cannot let it run me. First and foremost, I take time for myself. I have deadlines and I try to do all that is on my to-do list—but once I started to make myself a priority, I realized that I was able to give more to my daughter in our time together and I was more productive at work.

Making myself a priority ensures I get the sleep that I need and that I get the "me" time that I need. Sometimes I need to sit outside in nature and just be. And that's ok. Once I get this time to myself, I can better focus on everything else in my life. And you know what? Other people see it, they notice it, and they feel it. I am able to completely focus on what is in front of me and get things accomplished more quickly and efficiently than before. I have many peers tell me I am the calm, collected one who is able to support them when the atmosphere becomes overwhelming and chaotic. I can separate work completely from my home and social life. My time at work is focused on work. My time with my daughter is just that, and honestly, the first years of her life do not feel like they went by in a snap because I was fully present and completely enjoyed every moment I have had with her. My business has been created and run completely outside of these other worlds so that I can give my all to my clients. And in all of these times, if I feel that I need time for myself, I take it. And when I do that, I come back into what I was doing refreshed and re-energized.

When I first nurture myself, I am able to better nurture each and every person I spend time with. I know, again, easier said than done.

I have begun to show you how making yourself a priority is going to help you to give back more to yourself and others. It will also create a new sense of fulfilment for you. The big question is "How?" Like the everyday small steps I talked about in Chapter Five, prioritizing yourself will also be a small-step strategy. To change your mindset here is hard. You will be going against teachings, examples, and beliefs that are a part of you. You do not want to make this too much of a struggle for yourself so, to start the shift for you, you will need to focus on one area in your life where you feel you can start putting yourself first. Practice by integrating this small step into your lifestyle. Once this step is comfortable for you, truly comfortable, then you can add on another step. Again, here the process of step integration is very important. To avoid overwhelm—and to make lasting change—you must take it at a pace that allows you to sincerely add each step to a point where it does not feel like work but rather feels natural for you. At that point, you can build upon that step with another.

Your real success will depend on each step you are adding in and the fact that each one of these steps will need to feel right for you. Only you can decide what that will be. In Chapter Five, I asked you to reflect on what times of your routine already feel calm and peaceful. These activities could be one way to begin to prioritize you. Rose always lost herself when reading novels. She realized that when she was younger, she had read hundreds of novels, but as life began to take over with work and family, she let that go due to time constraints. She decided that her first step would be to take 15–30 minutes after dinner to read again. For many years, the time after dinner was for her to do household chores. She was now going to make a conscious commitment to take the first portion of that time for herself. This was a comfortable first step for her because she already knew the joy that reading brought to her. She still needed to consciously make the choice each night to do this, however, because she had a great sense of responsibility that was pulling her to finish her household chores.

Janine's first step was to begin to ask herself one question when she was making habitual choices throughout her day. The question she asked was, "Is this the choice Janine wants?" When she was in the deli in the morning to order breakfast, she was so used to getting the plain oatmeal with fresh fruit, that she just would grab it and go. When she made the commitment to ask herself this question, she decided to stop and contemplate this before following through with her usual morning ritual. As soon as she stopped and asked, she realized she truly did not want this breakfast. She became aware that this decision was being made because she felt it was the quickest, easiest, and healthiest choice for her at that moment. But now she realized she would actually rather have a vegetable omelet. The next day, she really felt like Greek yogurt with granola. She began to feel a sense of empowerment as she continued. She also realized that as she was honoring herself with what she truly wanted to eat for breakfast, she felt more confident and fulfilled going into her workday.

Over a simple choice like what to eat? Yes, it can be that small of a choice to start making lasting change.

Now, realistically, there are still responsibilities that need to be dealt with, whether you want to do them or not. My daughter must be picked up from school by 5:30, so I need to ensure that happens whether I want to do it or not. That's ok. I am not asking you to throw away responsibility—but I *am* asking you to reflect on decisions you are making, big and small, so that you become more aware of where your choices are coming from. Janine found when she asked this question of herself in situations at work, she would at times not be able to honor it. What did happen for her, however, was an awareness of what may be stressing her out versus what was bringing her peace and calm. When you are able to make choices that resonate more with yourself, you start to feel more confident in all that you are doing. You also feel like you are gaining back some control and you are not just going through the motions.

You will have different ways that work for you to get to a place where you are your own first priority. For many, this also will be a process that can bring up shameful feelings and guilt. Any process we go through will have roadblocks that I will talk through in the next pages. What you need to see is that making yourself the priority is not a selfish act and is not "bad." Doing this actually allows all the people in your life and the world around you to benefit at a level you never before realized was possible. As you start to shift to live this way, you begin to see the benefits, and you realize this is actually the most unselfish act you—as one human—could do, to help yourself and the world around you.

An additional level to prioritizing yourself and moving closer to your real success is to allow yourself to embrace your inner child. Who is that child inside? What are the thoughts of a young child? Excited to be alive, excited for what the world has to offer. No worries about what is to come. A child has big dreams and a desire to play through life. Can you rekindle this innocent playfulness? Can you imagine and dream big?

What you imagine can become real. Playfulness can bring joy and release. Embracing these attributes regularly will help you to further prioritize you. They will also help ease stress and tension associated with the everyday routine and mindset of responsibilities and requirements we place on ourselves.

You can make a conscious commitment to allow this inner child to reappear daily. Think about what aspect connects most with you when you are thinking of yourself as a child. If it is playfulness, for example, then allow yourself moment(s) of your day where playfulness is allowed to come out. Watch a cartoon, play a game, just allow yourself to remember and "daydream" of a time when you were playing as a child. Take what resonates with you the most, initially, and embrace it. Take small conscious steps and add it back in to your everyday being. It is never too late to embrace what it means to be true to yourself. Embracing your inner child is a great way to get closer to your true being.

What is your first small step to make yourself a priority?
What is your first small step to embrace your inner child?

Chapter Seven
Breakthrough

I have talked a lot about how we often live doing what we are supposed to do, following what we have been taught, allowing our conditioning to lead us. That conditioning makes up your internal belief system and creates your own subconscious and conscious rules about how you live your life. The everyday steps will help you to become aware, create focus, and allow you to better enjoy yourself in each moment. The re-prioritizing will create more space to nurture yourself, others, and the world around you. As you create these steps for yourself—and develop your ability to create space and allow for greater fulfillment— you will also begin to create a greater awareness of your own belief systems. This can cause you to begin to view your beliefs in a new light. As this happens, you may realize that there are certain conditionings that you already own that you now have a deeper connection to. You also may find some that you are now questioning.

Conditioning helps humans to have a structure. It can create rules, spoken or unspoken, that we live by to help keep order in society as a whole, within specific groups, or within our own minds. Society needs many rules. We are all taught at a very young age that red means stop. There are signs that are created in red to have us unconsciously register the need to stop. This is a benefit to our overall safety. We know that when we near a traffic light that is red, it means we need to stop our car. If we don't, we are jeopardizing our own and others' lives. This type of conditioning has our best interests in mind. Most conditioning is taught to you by someone or some entity that believes it is in your best interest to be taught it.

I have also mentioned that only you know what is right for you. Most likely you aren't even always 100 percent sure of what is right for you, but in the end only you have control over your own choices and actions, just as you alone have control over knowing what is right for yourself. As you go through life, you may start to see your beliefs differently as you experience new things. This can cause you to realize that a belief you formed is perfect for you or that it no longer serves you. As this happens, you start shifting your internal belief systems. But because you were conditioned by a person or group that you believed had your best interests in mind, or by an experience that you went through, once you challenge these beliefs, you may bring up many different feelings and emotions. Guilt, anxiety, overwhelm, fear—to name a few. This can stop you in your tracks and halt you from doing what is truly right for you. Maybe, you will decide that rather than face the reason you are feeling these emotions, you would rather just continue believing them. This option seems easier.

What will get you to face them more easily and confidently move through them? Motivation. Motivation is key for this entire process. Motivation allows you to make long-lasting shifts and choices. Because none of this is easy. If it was, we would all be at our own level of personal success and fulfillment, and this would not even be a topic of discussion for anyone.

I introduced you to Laura in Chapter Three. A single mom, teacher, and fitness instructor who was already questioning her beliefs when we started working together, Laura was motivated to make lasting change in her life. She was working just as hard on developing herself as she always had in every other area of her life. She felt that she had grown, but she kept hitting the same types of blocks over and over. She could not understand why she was not making inroads and she was exhausting herself in the process. She wanted change, and she wanted it yesterday. She was upset with herself that she had not done this work earlier, because she felt she had wasted a lot of time, and she also felt impatient that she knew where she needed to be, but she just could not get there.

Laura was able to realize in our work together that a lot of what she was looking at as needing change in her life was intertwined deeply with her belief system. This conditioning also was intertwined deeply with her emotions. Many of her issues—that she initially saw at surface level—were now intricate connections to a deeper subconscious belief system and she had no idea how to crack this open. But she was motivated, and she knew she had to do whatever work was necessary to move forward to where she knew she could and should be.

Laura became aware of conditioning that she had never before realized had been an internal driver for her. She started to understand how her daily emotional state was deeply rooted in the beliefs she held internally about herself, how she should look, who she should be and what she should have at this point in her life. Her subconscious conditioning was controlling her completely. Her emotions would rise up around these beliefs, and then her mind would take over and try to explain to her what was happening and why she felt this way. Her emotions were trying to tell her something and her mind kept fighting the emotions, so she was going in circles. She needed to create an awareness of the connections and then face them head on.

Laura lived her life creating and developing attachments to experiences and ideas she believed would satisfy her emotionally. She ended up associating emotions with these attachments. For example, she found herself in a cycle of bad relationships and she really felt stuck as to why she kept on attracting the same types of partners. Working together, she was able to pinpoint a want of security and intimacy as major points in what she felt comfortable with in relationships. She craved a feeling of being on a pedestal where her partner truly made her feel wanted through attraction and intimacy and by making her feel as if he would always support her through life's ups and downs. She also realized that she created attachments to past relationships where she had felt this way at points. Now she found herself having memories triggered in situations, such as visiting someplace she had gone with an ex. Once this occurred, she would have a flurry of emotion come up, and often a deep desire to return to her past because she craved this past feeling. This kind of emotional upheaval was happening very often, associated with different attachments she had made to external triggers in different areas of her life.

She became aware of the attachment to external sources and so began to fight herself as she would realize this was happening to her. This fighting, in turn, created chaos and overwhelm, and led her to make choices based on her mind chatter rather than what she truly needed or wanted. Hence her cycle kept repeating itself in different forms.

As we dug even deeper together, she was able to uncover self-beliefs that formed from a very young age. Her understanding of relationships and love was one. Here she was able to see that her belief of what these were was based on her own parents' relationship to each other and to her. She was not supported as a child emotionally, and so she craved the feeling of emotional support. She also saw connections from her childhood that led her to see intimacy and attraction as she did, due to her own self-loathing of her body and looks.

Laura had a lot to face and dig into, but she constantly moved forward. She first realized she needed to stop fighting herself when emotions came up. She created steps to allow herself to accept her emotions, so that she could stop beating herself up internally as soon as she felt them. She also started to reflect on her conditioning one belief at a time, to first understand where it stemmed from; second, accept that this is a subconscious or conscious belief for her; and third, decide if this belief truly resonated with her or not. Now one by one, she was able to start to face and possibly alter her conditioning on her own terms.

As you begin to create a new awareness of your belief system you will become more aware of how and why you may make daily choices in your life. You will begin to see how your thoughts are deeply connected to these subconscious rules you have formed. Suddenly, you will become more in tune with why your thoughts will fight you when you want to make a choice that your belief system does not connect to. These thoughts will create an internal struggle between your mind (and belief system) and your gut (or heart)—which knows what is really true for you. When this type of struggle is occurring internally, it can do many different things to you. Perhaps it will stop you from making any choice in the situation at hand. It could cause a continuing struggle and overwhelm and stress. If it truly is an important choice that you are faced with, it could lead to a constant mind overdrive that leads to sickness, anxiety, or even depressed feelings.

You may also start to realize that you have blocks and fears ingrained in your belief system that have developed through past experience. All of these things are holding you back from realizing your authentic success—and they too can be shifted to allow you to finally feel fulfilled.

You will realize your beliefs as well as blocks and fears that have been subconsciously controlling your choices. All of these can be altered or shifted to move you forward into fulfillment. Again, you can take small steps to begin your path toward breakthrough so that you may start to live life again on your terms.

So first, you must dig deep to uncover your internal beliefs, blocks, values, standards, and fears. Of course, you can do this on your own—and possibly, some of these are very apparent and come to mind immediately. If not, you can start asking yourself some questions to get yourself to reflect on this.

Let's practice this by first deciding on an area of your life you would like to focus on. Perhaps it's your career, or it could be your significant other and your relationship with them, your relationship with your parents, your self-image, or perhaps your financial status. Pick one and start asking yourself the following:

- Where am I concerning (chosen area) right now?
- In a perfect world, with no obstacles in my way, where would I be with (chosen area)?
- What are my current obstacles to realizing the perfect state with (chosen area)?
- Take each one of the obstacles from question 3 and reflect on how these obstacles are perhaps serving you right now.
- Now take each obstacle from question 3 and ask yourself, "If this was overcome, what would happen?"

This simple exercise can get your juices flowing to understand what may be preventing you from moving forward. Now you can go deeper. Take one of the obstacles that you answered in the third question and make that your chosen area to begin the process again. As you go deeper and more specific, you may be able to pick up on things that you had not originally connected to that area of your life.

Now, as you uncover connections to what has been leading your choices concerning specific areas of your life, what do you do with them?

You begin to add in small steps to your mindset to assist you to create change where you want it within the internal system that has been holding you back from realizing your authentic success.

There are many types of steps you could integrate into your life and mindset to start shifting your process. This is your personal journey and only you know what you want to move toward—so again this will be designed specifically for your needs and at your pace, on your terms.

I always had a belief that I needed financial security in the form of a good salary, benefits, and consistent paycheck. I did not believe that working for myself was secure enough, because at least with a salary I always knew the amount of income I was bringing home with each paycheck. I honestly never even questioned this belief until I hit my mid-thirties. Once it came up for me, and I went deeper, I was able to see that this formed from my childhood. I had a great home filled with love and support, but my parents constantly struggled financially. I had formed a sense of protection by holding onto the consistency of working for a corporate company that always gave me the same paycheck. This always felt right for me, but now I found myself questioning this. I realized this did not feel as good for me any longer.

But, I am a single mom and sole supporter of my daughter. I cannot let myself be reckless either. I went even deeper, and realized I had some insecurity about my ability to sustain a constant cash flow. As I reflected, I saw contradictions in my thought process. This led me to realize that I actually had a deep-rooted fear of losing everything and not being able to live. "But if I lost my income tomorrow what would I do?" I asked myself. And when I really broke it down, I knew I would be ok. I could create income pretty quickly and I have a fantastic support network in family and friends that I could lean on in the worst-case scenario. It would be a change, a struggle, but nothing close to the pit I felt in my stomach when first facing it without working it through.

I was able to pull my layers back one by one to expose deeper connections to my psyche and then face it head on. As I faced it, I was able to make lasting change in my belief since it no longer served me. This opened up a new pathway for me and allowed me to move forward with becoming an entrepreneur.

There are many ways that you can begin to pull layers back as you begin to dig deeper. You may realize that you need to quiet your mental chatter so that you can stop spinning and start refocusing. On another hand, you may realize that you have emotions connected to a large part of your internal process and you need to work on getting through these emotions to continue your journey.

Our inner voice is a large part of all of us. You often have a voice inside of you that helps direct you to the choices you make. Who is that voice in your head? If it is really you, then who is it actually talking to?

This is an interesting concept when you truly think about how this works for you internally. The voice is your mind. Your mind is telling you what it thinks. It is giving you advice. But what is this advice based on? It is based on your belief system. This is where conditioning is taking a large part in directing you. As you become more aware of this, and of the beliefs that are part of your inner thought process, this voice is not always so easy to listen to. You could do as Laura did and start arguing with this voice in your head at first. That would be an obvious first reaction when you are frustrated with what the voice is telling you. This, however, will cause more of a continuing cycle of the same frustrations arising over and over and can cause internal tension.

In my work with clients, I have seen this as an obstacle for most people. It can be a large reason why they are unable to move forward with what they are working on within themselves. As with the other areas I have told you about, this area also has many different types of steps and exercises that can be used to train your mindset so that this inner voice stops being a critic and starts to be a partner. You can stop just listening and doing what that voice has always been telling you, or start to partner with it and decide together on what the best course of action may be. Once you can create a new relationship with your inner voice, you will start to feel less overwhelmed with thoughts. This will add to your ability to begin to enjoy more of each moment, and to be able to make more decisions in the moment that will allow you to move forward in life with more fulfillment and ease.

So how do you add steps into your routine to create a better relationship with yourself—and create a partnership that allows you to live on your terms so that you may find your own fulfillment? There are many different steps that can be added, and you will have to decide what will resonate with you.

Rose, for example, had a binding agreement with her belief of being a perfect mom. She always allowed her critical internal voice to direct her until she became aware of her shift toward her belief system. Once this shift occurred, she found herself arguing with her internal voice and creating an overwhelming existence for herself, because her thoughts seemed to continue endlessly. She had intense feelings of guilt come up as she tried to break her ties to her old way of thinking. She knew she needed to change this process before she became sick from the undue stress she was experiencing. Her first step needed to be changing her reaction to the inner dialogue she continued to experience. Her current reaction of arguing and resistance was not allowing her to move forward. She decided she needed to first show herself compassion. Compassion would allow her to react to the inner dialogue from a different perspective. In order to do so, she first made the commitment to acknowledge her thoughts as they came up (Aware from the 3 As). If her inner voice would tell her, "Rose, you are going about this all wrong!" she would say back, "I understand that based on my initial view of what a perfect mom should be that you are right—I would be going about this wrong (Accept from the 3 As). Thank you for bringing that to my attention, but now we must figure out what I should do as a mentor rather than a mom who is doing it all for others (Allow from the 3 As)." She used this sparingly at first. When it felt comfortable to talk to herself this way, she moved forward doing so. Sometimes it would feel like a struggle to even consider this step and when it felt that way, she would tell herself, "It's ok Rose, you can face this again another time (Allow)." Talking back to herself with compassion started to allow her to feel good about the choices she was making even if they weren't always ones that would move her further on the path she was travelling. That was ok. As she started adding compassion in, she started to see her internal thoughts slow down and feel less forceful. This in turn led to less of a constant overdrive about the same things coming up over and over again. This was a perfect first step for Rose. She needed to consciously make herself aware of the compassion she needed for some time before it would start to just occur on a subconscious level.

Janine was trying to work on creating time for herself so that she could nurture herself and make space to have a social life and possibly find an intimate relationship. She found herself constantly fighting thoughts that would come up about her self-worth. She was never good enough and therefore did not deserve what she was craving. She was not a good daughter, sister, friend. She was not there for them for so long, why would they—or anyone—now be there for her. She also found that she thought she was not good enough for an intimate relationship. She was not good in other relationships, so how could she be good enough in a relationship that is so constant, personal, and intimate? She also had thoughts about not being good-looking enough or not having the personality that was good enough for another to fall in love with. Her thoughts kept telling her these things, so she started to feel and act as if these thoughts were the truth. She was motivated however to move forward, and she craved relationships. She needed to create a new relationship with her thoughts so that she could move to her next level. She decided that she needed to talk back to her internal thought process differently. She found it easier to visualize this thought process as a friend sitting across the table from her. As it told her these things, she then could create a conversation with it as if she was talking to another human being. This allowed her to create a new perspective on what was actually being said to her. She realized many of these thoughts were over-critical and unfounded. If another human being was making these statements to her, she would surely not be friends with that person. In fact, she would not allow an unhealthy relationship such as that to be any part of her life. This thought process made it easier for Janine to recreate her relationship with herself and stop the critical thoughts from taking over her attitude and sense of self.

Perhaps you have an overwhelm of thoughts, as Rose and Janine did, and need to create a course of action for yourself to get to a new level internally. And maybe you also have a deep emotional connection that you also realize leads you along. Emotions, like thoughts, can overtake you and cause you to make choices that are not truly aligned with yourself. Emotional dependence and reaction is another obstacle many face, and— as with the inner voice—this too can become a partnership rather than a struggle.

Laura realized that her emotions helped decide her actions. She also found that her moods throughout the day could be directly connected to one thought she had earlier. If she woke up and was getting ready for work and put on a pair of pants for the day that did not fit perfectly, all of a sudden, she would not feel good about herself. Initially she might feel disgusted or upset. She would move on to the rest of her day. As she would go through the day, she would realize she would become frustrated more quickly. Her patience would seem thinner, and she would often have random feelings of sadness or defeat. That one situation earlier was a deciding factor for her and how her emotional state would function as she moved on. She realized that when emotions came up for her, and she did not accept them and/or face them, they would sit in her subconscious and wreak havoc on her for at least the rest of the day, if not for a much longer period of time. She needed to do something about this!

Emotions can control you as much as your inner voice does, and when both partner together, they can veer you straight off course. Emotions should be used as guides. Feelings are great tools to understand what your conscious and subconscious are responding to and calling out. Laura realized that she had created attachments where specific emotions would arise when she would trigger a memory that she was connected to. This in turn was causing her to live focusing on past experiences and feelings rather than creating new memories with new emotions in the now. Laura's first step to move forward and break her dependence on attached emotions was to stop fighting them as they came up and start recognizing them (Aware) as well as accepting them. She had always fought so hard to try to suppress or fight the emotions because she knew she did not want to go back to her past. This ended up causing her to have the same emotions come up, over and over again, because she was not able to get past the initial cause. She was not facing the emotion because she was denying it. She needed to understand how to accept it. She started a process where, as an emotion would suddenly come up for her, she would first recognize it and next accept it. Similar to the process Rose took with her thoughts, Laura needed to start applying compassion to herself and her emotional state.

Laura was now taking the steps to acknowledge, or become aware of, the emotion, accept the emotion, and understand the emotion's reason for being—whether she agreed with it or not. This began to ease her everyday struggle of trying to control her emotions and now began to allow them to flow as they needed to. Once her first step began to ease her struggle, she was able to dig deeper and add more steps to start to shift how she was reacting to her emotional state overall. Once that shift took place, she began to see that her emotions were also changing. Her subconscious was starting to lessen its connection to past attachments.

Laura started to breakthrough. She began to move forward, feeling less burdened by her past and more free in the moment. She was able to stop using emotions as a crutch. As this happened, her mind started to slow down its thoughts as well. She truly began to feel that she was a partner with her mind, emotions, and inner being. Her days began to feel longer and more fulfilling. She was free to just be her and not the puppet she felt she was when her emotions had her by the strings.

What could happen for you once your thoughts and emotions are working in partnership with you? This partnership lessens the internal struggle that occurs within you. You start to feel as if you have more time and energy. Your life begins to flow more evenly, and you create more space for yourself to enjoy daily moments. You begin to feel a new level of accomplishment and fulfillment.

Questions to Ask to Assist in Uncovering Blocks, Fears, Beliefs:

- Where am I concerning (chosen area) right now?
- In a perfect world, with no obstacles in my way, where would I be with (chosen area)?
- What are my current obstacles to realizing the perfect state with (chosen area)?
- Take each one of the obstacles from the third question and reflect on how these obstacles are perhaps serving you right now.

Now take each obstacle from the third question and ask yourself, "If this was overcome, what would happen?"

Chapter Eight
What It Looks Like Now

When I first start working with clients, and I ask them where they see themselves right now, they usually say things like stressed, overwhelmed, unfulfilled. They believe they just need more time and more energy. They often feel that they are happy with many of the choices they have made because they have followed the path they felt was right for them. They feel as if they are, and always have been, controlling their path and in doing so, have set goals and put a plan in place to get them to where they will live life with a larger sense of joy. They are also at a point where they are not as far along as they always believed they would be in finding that joy, and are now even further committed to getting there because they feel they do not want to waste any more time.

What we often find as we go deeper, is that they have actually been putting themselves into a type of box by constantly pushing for something that is already right in front of them. They want this overall end of complete joy, but they are focused at the moment on a big picture goal such as getting a promotion at work. Is that promotion truly the big picture? Will that promotion alone, bring them full joy? No. And will the next promotion or the next $10k in income get them there? How about meeting their soulmate? These are all small pieces to a larger puzzle that look great to us. But as we add these pieces, there are still so many more pieces we are still searching for. These are all external factors as well. So, once we accumulate all that we are striving for on the outside, do they guarantee our complete joy on the inside?

Right now, you are working hard. You are doing everything you are supposed to be doing. You are accomplishing goals, and you are successful by doing so. You are taking steps every day to ensure that you and the world around you are moving in the right direction. You may feel that you are proud of how far you have come and what you have been able to accomplish in life so far. You may also feel that there is so much more you strive to bring to yourself, your loved ones, and the world as a whole. And, if you can get to that top level you will finally feel fulfilled.

This working hard and accomplishing one external goal at a time is the traditional way of going through life. So, what if you break the mold a bit and—rather than having complete focus on the next goal that you believe you must achieve—you begin to allow yourself to focus on what is actually inside of you and in front of you?

I knew with every ounce of my being that I would create my business. No question about it. I did not write up a plan and go step by step. I honestly never thought about all of the steps I needed to take to get it started, let alone to develop it to a higher level. And, nowhere in my thoughts was writing a book. Yet here I am writing, and I feel fabulous as I am doing so, knowing that I am putting these ideas out into the world so that others can benefit. This was never a next step for me, it was never an overall goal, it just happened. In fact, the entire business was never a goal for me until the moment I just knew it would exist. The only reason any of this came to life for me was because I started living a life where I allowed what was right in front of me to unfold. I stopped doing what I was supposed to do just to prove myself to the world. I began to do what truly felt right for me. And since I have started living this way, I have accomplished so much, and I feel so much more fulfilled. I am giving back to the world in a way I had never before imagined and I know that I will continue and grow as I continue. And I have no expectations outside of my knowing that I will always live my life achieving my real success.

This is what you deserve. You deserve to feel this way every day and with every moment. And you can.

What could this look like for you?

What does it look like when you are living your real success?

Perhaps you are able to work on yourself to be able to live life in the moment rather than always striving for the next best thing, and all of a sudden, opportunities you have never even dreamt of start to present themselves to you. Once you begin to implement your own plan, and adjust yourself to live with fewer expectations, you may find that life finally gets to a level of fulfillment you never even imagined could exist.

You may find that you are in your dream job and so you continue that path, but at the same time, you find opportunities to expand your life at home. All of a sudden, the to-do list is no longer a struggle, because you are getting everything accomplished with ease. And you finally feel that you are now experiencing your moments with yourself and your family rather than just getting everything done in time. On the other hand, perhaps at home you are already fully satisfied with your relationships and the way you allocate yourself and your time. Your finances are the only thing holding you back from truly feeling fulfilled. As you release your expectations, you find that money begins to flow in more easily for you in ways you never could have planned yourself. As you start to live life without a constant burden on your shoulders, the world begins to offer you more.

Sandy had begun by shifting her attitude through listening to music on her drive home. She continued to take steps to add calm into her routine and life. She had been struggling at her career for some time, as she was working in a very toxic environment. In her process, she was not focused on making any changes there yet. She was adding steps into her lifestyle away from that. As she continued her path, she suddenly was offered an opportunity for a new job, exactly what she wanted to do, near her home and at a higher salary. She was not looking for it. She didn't realize she was even ready for that step at that moment—but once it was presented to her it truly felt right. It felt right for her, no one else, and she took it. She was ecstatic over receiving this opportunity once it was in front of her, but she had no expectation of it until it was right there.

This is what begins to happen for you as you create this new way of being. And, all of a sudden, life flows much more fluidly. Thoughts and emotions do not continue to rule your next steps. Will you continue to have goals? Yes. But you will begin to move toward them with less expectation and attachment, and possibly those goals will change completely or evolve into something else because you begin to honor yourself truly.

This process and the outcome will be unique to each of us. It will happen as it needs to for you. You will focus on what you need to focus on—not what the world expects you to. Because it is so unique, there is no one way to go. You need to decide each step for yourself so that you can move forward confidently and in a way that will allow you to make lasting change.

Chapter Nine
Don't Get Pulled off Track

I was just watching a Mickey Mouse movie with my daughter and in it, Mickey states: "I would need a sorcerer if I ever wanted to clean up this mess!" That is exactly what this process is! The sorcerer to finally bring you to where you deserve to be. As I mentioned, this process transformed me and brought me to a place where I am accomplishing things I never even before had imagined. It created my business. It created this book. It has allowed me to serve countless others. But I do want to make sure you know this was not an overnight transformation. For me to get here was a process that was not free of bumps. I wanted to present this process to you because the outcomes it provides are spectacular, but I also want to make sure you can do it successfully. So that you can be successful, I want to make you aware of some things that could possibly take you off track or cause some hiccups. By being aware of these, you can have a better sense of when you may need support, and when you may need to ask for help.

One way that you can push yourself off track is by moving too fast. We live in an extremely fast-paced world where we have access to almost anything at our fingertips. Therefore, most of us want things done quickly. This process is not something that can be rushed. I had compared it to training for a race earlier. You can also compare it to your own need to heal. If you break a bone, you cannot speed up its recovery. You may try to use it sooner, and then it ends up getting re-injured and the healing time actually gets extended. The same thing will happen here. You need to take the time to allow yourself to adjust before you add on and overwhelm yourself. If you push too soon, you can set yourself behind and the overall process will become longer than it could have been. A client I am working with right now, Sophie, is extremely driven. She has always gotten everything done before her deadlines. Her whole entire life she has been the one who completes each task and goal before anyone else, and well before her own internal deadlines. All of this speed and rushing has caught up to her and she is at a point, as she says, "where she needs to stop and smell the roses." Slowing down is a very hard process for her, however, and she found herself trying to rush her own process to get to the finish line sooner. She was adding steps into her routine to try to create more awareness of what was going on in front of her. Initially, she decided her first step would be to spend her time eating dinner completely focused on her family in front of her. She would focus on conversation and just being there together. Once this was feeling comfortable to her, she decided to add the same process to her daily meeting with her colleagues at the office. All seemed to be moving smoothly, but she was having a tough time taking it so slowly and decided instead that she would add the same process to every meeting with colleagues and clients as well as to after dinner time with her family.

She suddenly began to feel anxious and overwhelmed. She was using so much energy trying to consciously stay focused, during large amounts of her day, that she started to spin when dealing with everything that needed to be accomplished. During our next session together, she was unfocused and unclear on where she was, let alone where she needed to go next. I supported her pulling herself back so that she could slowly make conscious decisions, that in time, would shift her subconscious. She had created a situation of angst for herself by trying to move too quickly and she lost some ground on the work she had already begun to accomplish. Luckily for her, this surfaced pretty quickly, and she was able to get herself back on track. She was working toward adding calm and focus into her routine, and she ended up feeling chaotic and lost by pushing too hard too quickly.

Another obstacle that can come up is believing you should be somewhere that you are not yet. You may start to judge yourself, as you begin to consciously make adjustments to the way you are thinking. In this process, you begin to create a deeper level of awareness of yourself and to your internal processes. Once you see these processes more clearly, you may have thoughts and emotions surface because you become upset with yourself for still reacting in ways you know you need to shift. This could be associated with a want to adjust quickly, as I spoke about above, or it could be that, because you have started to shift your belief system in your awareness, you become angry with yourself when you do things subconsciously as you had done them in the past. Once you start beating yourself up about not accomplishing something, you begin to take yourself away from the moment you are in. You also may start to awake the inner critic, who will begin to berate you for your actions. All of a sudden, you are taking away your focus and you are using your energy to yell at yourself for something that is now in the past and cannot be changed. As this is allowed to develop, it puts you into overdrive mentally and emotionally, and you begin to lose ground on being able to move forward.

Here, we need to meet ourselves with compassion. Instead of reacting to yourself with anger or frustration, you can lead with love.

Laura would make such great strides in her process. She had created such a deep awareness of what was driving her emotionally. She was able to understand where an emotion was rising from much more easily. She was very happy with the progress she had made in this area. She still would have the emotions arise as her day went on, however. This made her mad. She was so aware of them, she completely understood what the emotion was related to and why it had come up for her, so why, with this awareness, was she still dealing with it all day long? She would find herself then becoming engulfed in thoughts. Chatter would flood her mind about how she was not moving forward, and she should be. This created an internal struggle for her that would take her away from the focus and awareness she had developed and bring her back into an internal fight that would feel as if she was taking herself backward.

Laura realized she needed to be compassionate with herself. She was growing so much internally, she needed to be fair to herself and the process. And pure awareness of an emotion, and where it was coming from, was not enough. She needed to start to tell herself that she accepts the emotion. She understands that it is coming from her old conditioning that she is now trying to shift, and that is ok. Now that she is able to be aware of it, understand its origins, and accept that it still resides in her as it does, she can move forward facing it, rather than fighting it. This was a huge obstacle for Laura. Because she had been beating herself up, she truly felt she was making no progress. Once she began to meet herself with compassion, she stayed calm and focused on where she needed to lead herself next to shift her internal beliefs.

Awareness is a major piece of this process. As you shift your mindset to focus on what is happening in the moment, you will create an awareness of many new things. Your awareness of the external world will develop tremendously. You will notice little things you would never have before. The same is true for yourself internally. Your way of being, your attachments, your beliefs, your emotions, and your thoughts will all be seen in a new sense of awareness. Because this begins to happen, you may start to find things that you never knew were there. You can become scared, anxious, guilty, or angry as things begin to surface. This is all normal. But as your awareness expands and these feelings come up, they may bring up beliefs, fears, and blocks that you never realized existed or that are not comfortable for you. Again, this is all part of the process. However, if you decide to put up walls to these because they are not sitting with you right, or you just have no idea what to do with them or where they came from, you will cause unnecessary internal turmoil, tension, and struggle. Once you create a struggle inside, it will continue to block you from moving to your next level until it is faced and dealt with.

Rose, as I mentioned, was aware completely of her shift in her belief of what a perfect mom was. She kept on feeling a great deal of guilt as she tried to move forward on her path, however. She did not know why she was feeling so much guilt, and she really did not like the feeling it gave her. So, she tried to just push it away. The more she was pushing it away, the stronger it was getting. She finally felt it so often, and so strongly, that she had to do something about it. It was making her thoughts go into overdrive and making her sick. She was also feeling stuck where she was in her process overall. Rose needed to face this feeling. She needed to stop pushing it away, and truly understand where it was coming from. Rose was able to peel off some layers, to truly reach to where this was coming from internally, and as she did, she was able to actually gain true understanding and put compassion toward her guilt, so that she could in turn transform it within her. Once she was able to do this, she felt a weight had been lifted and she could now move forward again.

One more obstacle that could come up for you is that you believe that once you hit a milestone, then that's it—you're good to go. It is so great to feel accomplishment, as we know, but one thing you need to know as you embark on this journey is that this is a process that will continue indefinitely. You are consciously training yourself to subconsciously act in a new way. You will continue to evolve for the rest of your life. You may right now truly just be concerned with getting to the next level in your career. That's great if that is what you want. As you begin this process, that next level may begin to happen for you. Because that short-term goal is met, however, does not mean you have aced this process. If you decide to stop once a short-term goal is met, you may just end up in the same state next year. Once that happens, you will realize you need to restart this process to truly shift.

As mentioned, there are various obstacles that can stand in our way as we create our real success. Moving too quickly, judgment, guilt, anger, and anxiety are all obstacles we may face. Also, beliefs, fears, and blocks may surface that can take us off course. Many tools were given throughout the book to help you through these on your own. The Real Success Strategy itself helps us through many of these. Also, just the awareness of the fact that these obstacles exist can help you move through them more quickly. In the next chapter, we will look at next steps and how you can support yourself to create your real success as easily and efficiently as you are able.

Chapter Ten

Next Steps

*L*aura is one of my clients who was working so hard on herself prior to coming to me. She had grown tremendously in the few years leading up to when she decided to reach out for my support. She was investing in herself so that she could have the life she craved, and she was seeing herself make strides to get there, but she also felt that something was blocking her from getting to where she knew she could be. She had expended a lot of time and energy on her personal development and now she felt she was stuck. She needed support and accountability to pull her through and she was willing to invest in herself to get to the point she wanted to be. Are you, like Laura, ready to reach your next level? Are you motivated to shift your life to one of greater fulfillment?

If your answer is a resounding yes, let's look at what we have covered together so far so you can begin implementing this process and creating your new reality.

What is your *real success*?

I filled you in on a way to understand truly what it is you are craving, to finally begin to live the life you have been striving to: Your Real Success. What does life look like when you have achieved this real success? What does it look like when you stay where you are?

What's happening?

Most of us believe we are following the path we are supposed to, to get ahead and achieve success. We continue to do what we are supposed to do because it is the "good" thing to do.

The Real Success Strategy:
We can begin to apply the 3 As method into our lives.

Awareness

Acceptance

Allowance

We can take small steps to begin to feel our real success in all areas of our lives: physically, emotionally, and mentally. We will apply this method in:

- Our everyday small steps
- Our priorities
- Our breakthroughs

As we shift these areas of our lives in ways that resonate and work for each of us, individually, we begin to feel our real success more and more each day. We begin to live the life we deserve to be living.

This is a process and a strategy. It does not happen overnight, and it is not free of bumps and roadblocks.

So now the choice is yours. Do you want to continue on the path that you are expected to be on, continue to work hard and achieve success the traditional way, or do you want to step into a version of yourself that is finally finding fulfillment by honoring yourself rather than the expectations placed on you? Now, I am not saying that the latter path will be easy. But it will get you to a new level of fulfillment. How will you feel in two years when you find yourself living life at a higher level of fulfillment? One where you are living your authentic success rather than just craving it?

You are moving through your daily routine with a new sense of freedom. Life is not passing you by like a whirlwind. You feel just as accomplished making small choices as you do making the large ones. You feel at peace and you are loving every second of it.

I wish this for you in every way. And I know you can have this. You are passionate and determined. You are already someone who accomplishes and moves ahead. Now you can move ahead on this path.

The decision is yours.

- What is your real success?
- What does life feel and look like when you are living that real success?

- What does life feel and look like if you do not create your real success?

You can just read this book and apply this process and get yourself to a higher level of fulfillment and a life of authentic real success. I have given you the 3 As method, the overall concepts, and the generalized tools to implement to do so. For some, this book will be enough. They will take this book and implement it in the way that works best for themselves and they will move toward this new level of fulfillment. For others, they will take a piece of what they were given in this book and implement it, and they will make some changes in their well-being. Again, they will make the changes that resonated with them. For many, they will try to implement it all and they will not end up where they want to be. They may end up feeling stuck at points, or alone and in need of support. Please, if this is you, seek out help. Laura did this and now she is further along than she would have been staying stuck. She was actually at a point where she was beginning to walk backward on her path of growth. If she did not seek the help and support she needed at that point, she could have created more chaos and overwhelm than before she started. Now, she is on a path that is easier and quicker than she had even imagined possible. There are many places you can seek out support and accountability. What matters is that the place you are getting it from is right for you. This entire process will only work as you honor yourself and what you truly need.

So where does this leave you now? I have shown you that you can start living a more fulfilling life by shifting to this real success mindset. Yes, this shift of mindset is a process and it needs to be done at the pace that is right for you, and in ways that resonate with you. You can begin this process right now—if you are motivated to. Possibly, you are not sure where to start, but you are very motivated to implement this process for yourself. Honor your feelings first. Understand truly what feels right to you, and you can take the next step. If you had something resonate with you in this book that you would like to try to implement right away, you can do that. If you want to dive right into the process and you know in your heart you need support, feel free to connect with me. I would like everyone to benefit from this process. I am happy to talk to you about your path and what would be best for you. If I am not the fit that you need for support, I would be honored to be able to give you suggestions or referrals should I be able to.

In the end, I want you to achieve your real success and I am honored to have been at least a stepping stone on your path to fulfillment.

Acknowledgments

I am eternally grateful to the universe for blessing me with the life I have been given and that I am eternally growing and changing. I am in complete gratitude that I have been able to support others on their paths to become who they truly are. My passion is to pass this on to as many as will accept it, and my choice to create my business and write this book was for one purpose—to allow this message to reach as many people as it can.

None of this would have been possible if I did not have the support and love I have been blessed with. First my mother, Susan, you are beyond any words. Your love is what brought me here and you continue to support and love me in unlimited ways. I thank the universe for you every day. This book would have not been written had you not been here for me. My father, Ron, you have always been there for myself and my Valerie, thank you. My best friend and sister, Heather—thank you for being you.

To the Morgan James Publishing team: Special thanks to David Hancock, CEO & Founder for believing in me and my message. To my Author Relations Manager, Margo Toulouse, thanks for making the process seamless and easy. Many more thanks to everyone else, but especially Jim Howard, Bethany Marshall, and Nickcole Watkins.

Finally, to my Valerie, thank you for lighting up my life every day. May you continue to live your life with the passion, energy, and love you are leading with now. Thank you for reminding me to shine bright every day.

About the Author

Michelle Zawaski believes we are all striving for the same end but each in our own unique way. Her passion is people and their infinite capacity to grow and evolve. She was born into this world with this passion but was swept into following the path that she was taught would get her ahead in society. She was able to rediscover herself through life experiences that motivated her to create methods that brought her back to her own personal success and fulfillment. Now she is using these same tools to help others achieve the success they too have been striving for. She became an entrepreneur, coach, author, and motivator so that she could support others in their pursuit of personal success and fulfillment.

Michelle is a certified professional coach through Life Purpose Institute. She has spent most of her life coaching and supporting others and she understands that no single approach can work for all. For the last few years, she has been able to focus completely on each motivated individual and what they need for their own unique path to personal success. She created tools and techniques that can be used in ways that work for each person so that they may grow at the pace that fits for them.

Michelle lives in Queens, NY, with her daughter. She enjoys learning and growing from each person that she crosses paths with. She spends as much time as she can with her daughter, family, and friends. She loves being in nature and soaking up as much sunlight (and moonlight) as possible.

Website: michellezawaski.com
Email: michelle@michellezawaski.com
Facebook: https://www.facebook.com/mzawaski/

Thank You

I truly want to thank you for reading this book. I know that you are committed to finding your Real Success so that you can start living every moment feeling accomplished and realizing true fulfillment.

If you are ready to jump in and make Real Success your reality now, go to michellezawaski.com/apply to set up time for A *Free* Real Success Strategy session so we can talk about how you can get there.

CPSIA information can be obtained
at www.ICGtesting.com
Printed in the USA
BVHW032017240719
554243BV00018B/35/P

9 781642 792386